THE COCOON
& THE BUTTERFLY

THE COCOON
& THE BUTTERFLY

ELISABETH KÜBLER-ROSS, M.D.

EDITED BY GÖRAN GRIP, M.D.

STATION HILL OPENINGS

BARRYTOWN, LTD.

Published under the Station Hill Openings imprint by
Barrytown, Ltd., Barrytown, N.Y. 12507.

Distributed by Consortium Book Sales & Distribution, Inc.
1045 Westgate Drive, Saint Paul, MN 55114-1065.

Text and cover design by Susan Quasha.

The talk in this book has been excerpted from *Death is Of
Vital Importance*, Copyright by Elisabeth Kübler-Ross, Station Hill Press, 1995.

A Swedish version of *Death is Of Vital Importance* has been
published by Bokförlaget Natur och Kultur under the title
Döden är livsviktig: Om livet, döden och livet efter döden,
Copyright 1991 by Elisabeth Kübler-Ross.

Library of Congress Cataloging-in-Publication Data

Kübler-Ross, Elisabeth.
    The cocoon & the butterfly / Elisabeth Kübler-Ross ;
edited by Göran Grip.
            p.   cm. – (Kübler-Ross in person)
    Excerpted from: Death is of vital importance, 1995.
    ISBN 1-886449-25-2 (lg. Print)
    1. Death.   2. Life.   3. Future life.   4. Spiritual life.
I. Grip, Göran.   II. Title.   III. Series: Kübler-Ross, Elisabeth.
Kübler-Ross in person.
    [BD444.K78   1997]
    155.9'37—dc21   96-48562
                                                     CIP

Printed in the United States of America.

Contents

ABOUT THIS BOOK

Elisabeth Kübler-Ross' words, spoken at the spur of the moment, have been edited here with the aim of creating a readable text. We have taken pains, however, to preserve the quality of immediate presence that is characterized by the author's special magnetism, the power of direct address to a live audience for which she is renowned. We think there is a special meaning in presenting Elisabeth Kübler-Ross "live" on the subject of death and dying — and that this is a key to her message.

This book has been adapted from Elisabeth Kübler-Ross' tape-recorded lecture, delivered in Sweden, in 1981 (Second Stockholm Lecture).

The Cocoon &
the Butterfly

The first time I was here in Sweden was 1947. A lot of things have changed since then. If anybody would have told me in 1947 what I'd be doing today, I don't know whether I would have had the courage to get started.

Two days ago I was in Duisburg, and the first thing that greeted me was those people with the big signs about bomb threats and bomb detection machines. I wondered why people feel so threatened by somebody who works with dying children.

I will talk very briefly as a psychiatrist to help you understand the main lessons that we have learned from working with dying patients. Dying patients not only teach us about the process of dying but also what we can learn about how to live in such a way that we have no unfinished business.

People who have lived fully will be afraid neither of living nor of dying. And to live fully means that you have no unfinished business, and that in turn means that you have to be raised in a way very few of us and our children have been raised. I am sure that if we had one generation of children that were raised in a natural way, the way we were created, we would not need to write books on death and dying and have seminars and have these horrendous problems with one million children disappearing and thousands of them dying prematurely by suicide and homicide.

The Four Quadrants

Spiritual/ intuitive Adolescence	Physical Birth-1 year
Intellectual 6-13 years	Emotional 1-6 years

Every human being consists of four quadrants: a physical, an emotional, an intellectual and a spiritual/intuitive quadrant.

When we are born, we are exclusively **physical** human beings, and during the first year of life, in order to grow up in a natural way, afraid neither of living nor of dying, we need a lot of loving, hugging, touching and physical contact. Then at the end of our life, when we are old Grandmas or Grandpas living in nursing homes, then again the one aspect of our life that we are missing the most is that we are not touched, loved and hugged enough. In our society the only people usually who give us totally unconditional love were the very old people: our Grandmas and Grandpas.

In a society where every generation lives all by themselves — the old people in nursing homes, sick people in hospitals, children at school — most children miss that aspect of growing up. And that gives the children their first problems in the development of their **emotional** quadrant (between the ages of one and six) where they get all their basic attitudes that will mark them for life.

Our children need to be raised with unconditional love and firm consistent discipline, but with no punishment. That sounds easy, but it is not easy. But it *is* possible to dislike their behavior and still love them. If you are able to do that, the children develop a very beautiful **intellectual** quadrant at around the age of six; they love to learn, and going to school is a challenge, not a threat.

My big dream before I die is to start E.T.-centers. And that is to change old age homes into E.T.-centers. Is there anybody here who has not seen the movie, "E.T."?

E.T.-centers are homes for the Elderly and Toddlers. You skip one generation. You will have no problems. The old people who have contributed to society for seven decades are entitled to have a home of their own — a nice, private place with their own furniture — and they would live on the first floor. And the only payment they would have to make would be to take care of one child and spoil that child rotten. They would have to pick a child who appeals to them the most from among the toddlers of working parents. The parents will bring them in in the morning when they go to work and pick them up at the end of the day.

The gift that they give to each other would be of mutual benefit. The old people would be touched again. Little children love wrinkled faces. They even like pimples. They play piano on them *(laughter from audience)*. And old people need more hugs and touches and kisses — especially from children. The children in the first few years of their lives would learn total, unconditional love. If you have lived with unconditional love early in life, things can get very bad later on in life, and you will still be able to cope with it. If you have experienced unconditional love once, it will last for your whole lifetime. It does not have to be from your father or your mother, who may not be capable of giving it, because they them-

selves have never received it. That is my
E.T.-center dream.

In adolescence you would very naturally develop your **spiritual, intuitive**
quadrant. This is how we would develop
normally and naturally, if we were per-
mitted a natural evolution through growing up with no interference. The spiritual,
intuitive quadrant is that part of you that
has all knowledge. It is the only quadrant in the human being that we do not
need to work for, because we are born
with it. We are also given a gift: if we lose
something we always get something in
return that is better than the part we lost.
In children who die at a young age of leukemia, brain stem tumor, or what have
you, the physical quadrant deteriorates.
The gift that they receive in its place —
and we grownups do not appreciate this
enough — is that their spiritual quadrant
begins to emerge, sometimes already at
the age of three, four or five. The longer
they have suffered and the more they
have suffered, the sooner this evolves.
They will look like tiny children — much

younger than their chronological age —
but their spiritual quadrant is so wide
open that they talk like old, wise people.

These children come to this earth to be
our teachers. If we do not hear them, if
we pretend that they are too young to
know about dying, or if we play games
with them, then *we* are the losers, not the
children.

The problem is that very few of us are
totally intuitive, that most of us do not
listen to ourselves, but listen to others to
tell us what to do. And that is because
most of us were raised with conditional
love. If you have been raised with, "I love
you if you bring good grades home," "I
love you if you make it through high
school," "God, would I love you if I could
say: my son the doctor," then you have
been raised with the belief that you can
buy love, that your parents will love you
if you become what your parents want
you to become. And you end up becom-
ing a prostitute *(scattered laughs from audience)*. Prostitution is the biggest problem in this world because of this one

word, "if." There are millions of people who would do anything, anything in the world, to make sure that their parents love them. Anything. Those are the people who believe that you can buy love. They shop around until the end of their lives, shopping for love, and they never find it. Because you cannot buy real love. And they are the ones I see on their death bed saying very sadly to me, "I have made a good living, but I have never really lived." Then you ask them, "What does it mean to you to really live?" And they say, "Well, I was a very successful lawyer, or a very successful doctor, but I really wanted to be a carpenter."

—————

When you work with dying patients, first you exclusively take care of their physical needs, their physical quadrant. You will have to keep your patients first and foremost pain free. Physical comfort and absence of pain comes long before any emotional support, before any spiritual help, before anything else. You cannot help a dying patient emotionally or spiritually if he is climbing up the wall with pain, or if you on the other hand give him pain injections that make him so dopey and sedated that he cannot communicate any longer.

And so what we do is to give the patients an oral pain cocktail that is given before they have any pain, and that is given to them regularly, so that they always are pain free and conscious until the moment they die. All this is a pre-requirement for emotional support.

When they are comfortable physically, pain free, not left alone, dry and able to communicate, then you move on to the emotional quadrant.

But how do you communicate with a terminally ill patient who cannot say a word? How do you communicate with a patient who has ALS or has had a massive stroke and is totally paralyzed up to here? How do you ever figure out that he, for example, wants you to scratch his back? You are not mind readers — very few people are — so how do you communicate with him? Well, you make a speaking board: you make a list of the alphabet, a list of all the important persons, a list of all the body parts, then a list of all the important physiological needs. Then even a ten year old child can go up and down on these lists and the patient can go "Hrrr" when he points at the right word or the right letter.

This speaking board is a God-given gift for ALS patients. It has not all that worth for stroke patients because many of them cannot comprehend written words. So for stroke patients, you will have to make a board of pictures instead.

It is important that you know about the speaking board, because if a patient is totally intelligent and lies on his back for four years and cannot communicate with you in any way, then you will begin to treat him like he is deaf and dumb because there is no response coming from him. And people disconnecting from you is one of the worst deaths you can experience.

I had a consultation a few years ago requested by the wife of a middle aged man who had been paralyzed and unable to speak for four years.

When I saw the patient, he was a very devastated man lying flat on his back. He had two small children and a *very* exhausted wife. And all he could express was total panic.

I used a speaking board and asked him why he was in such a panic and he answered that his wife was trying to get rid of him. I said, "She is trying to get rid of you? But she has been taking care of you for four years day and night, twenty-four hours a day!" He said, "Yes. That's why she is trying to get rid of me. She has had it. She cannot take any more and she has made arrangements to send me to a hospital." Now he was afraid that in the last few weeks of his life, she would send him off to a hospital, and he knew hospitals well enough to know that they would put him on a respirator.

He said that for four years he had been watching his children grow up, and that he was able to cope with his disease. And now in the last few weeks of his life, he said, his wife couldn't take it any more and wanted him to go to the hospital. He begged her to please hang in there another couple of weeks, and he promised her to die soon, so that it would not be such a burden on her.

I asked her right in front of the patient and the children if he was right, and she confirmed that she had made arrangements to make the hospital take him because she was at the end of her physical strength. All of you who have ever taken care of a patient twenty-four hours a day know that no human being can do that for four years. And I asked her what it would take to hang in there another few weeks. Because if a patient who is *not* neurotic tells you that he has only a couple of weeks to live, then you should listen to him!

And she said, to make a long story short, that she needed a man. And I asked her if it was that difficult to live without a man. And she said no, she had gotten used to not having a husband, but the reason she needed a man was that she needed a strong person who could take over the night shift from 8 P.M. to 8 A.M., so she could sleep through a whole night. I think that any one of you who have had a sick child knows that this is a very reasonable request.

I believe that there are no coincidences in life — I call them "divine manipulations." I knew that I made this house call the night before a five-day workshop and I said, "You know, I'm sure I'm here because in this workshop will be *just* the right man. And I will kidnap him and bring him here *(amusement from audience)* to take over your night shifts. And just in case this does not happen, I will come back and make another house call."

And this woman had so much faith in what I call divine manipulation that she said she would hang in there for another five days.

Then the workshop started. We always have more women than men, naturally. I only looked at the men *(amusement from the audience)*. I looked at every man in this group of one hundred people. I said to myself, "Maybe that's the man? No. Maybe him? No." Nobody looked right.

And by Wednesday I started to get nervous *(amusement from audience)*. Usually my intuition is very good. It's when I use my head that I get into trouble *(amusement from audience)*. But by Wednesday I looked at every man except the one who had not yet shared.

And then this man came up and he started to share, and at the *moment* he opened his mouth I said, *"No way* is he going to take care of this patient." He talked, if you excuse the expression, like a Californian *(laughter from audience)*. That's a nasty expression, I don't mean it nasty. He was sitting like... folded up *(tries to demonstrate how he was sitting)*. I can't sit that way.

He shared how he went from workshop to workshop from Esalen to the Himalayas. He lived on brown rice and raw vegetables *(amusement from audience)*. I cannot describe him more grotesquely, but he was one of these *real* extremists *(amusement from audience)* who had workshopitis *(laughter from audience)* and I regard these people as parasites because they never work, they just go from workshop to workshop *(laughter)*. And the more he talked the more I said, "No, no, no. I can't send such a person to this man."

And at the end of his sharing he said, "I want to go in your footsteps. I want to do this kind of work." And I thought, "I'm gonna show you." *(amusement from audience)* I said, "Are you willing to work twelve hours a day?"

"YES!"

"Are you willing to work with a man who can't speak?"

"Yes!"

"Who can't write notes?"

"Yes!"

"Day and night?"

"Yes!"

"Are you willing not to get paid for your work?"

"Yes!"

The worse I described the patient the more excited he got *(amusement from audience)*. And at the end I had no way out but to tell him, "OK. Your work starts at Friday night 8 P.M." *(laughter from audience)*

I must say that I had absolutely no expectations that he would show up at work. I thought, "When the workshop is over at noon Friday, he will disappear."

But he not only started to work for this family, he did the best job anybody has ever done for any of my patients. From foot massage to cooking special meals, to reading to the patient. He was *really* taking care of him. And he stayed until two weeks after his death to be sure that the family was OK.

And the lesson *I* learned is never to underestimate a Californian *(big laughter form audience)*. You never, ever, ever . . . Any time you react negatively to a person or to anything you must understand that this is your own unfinished business. Do you hear that? I reacted much longer than fifteen seconds to that man, so I had to go home and look at what turns me off when I hear about brown rice and raw vegetables *(laughter from audience)*. That's because I drink coffee and eat hamburgers and smoke cigarettes and I am very allergic to this extremist health food stuff *(amusement from audience)*. But that's the way you diagnose your own unfinished business. And it is very important that you do that.

So after you take care of the physical needs of your patient, after you have been sure that there is a way to communicate — and there is never no way to communicate if you know about the speaking board — then only is it possible to take care of the emotional quadrant.

All you need to do as a helper is to ask what you can do for them and hear and listen to the dying patients who tell you, from their intuitive quadrant, not from their intellectual quadrant, what it is that they need to do in order to live, literally to live, until they die.

But you have to be aware of the fact that many, many patients share with you that they *don't* want your help. They tell you in a polite and sometimes in a not very polite way that you should go home, what are you doing here?

Most people who offer their help feel terribly rejected when they are told to go home. But you have to appreciate that if you were dying and you were in a hospital and somebody came and offered to help you finish your unfinished business you would say, "No thank you!" because you would like to choose your own friend with whom to finish unfinished business and you would not like a hospital administrator to send someone in to do it for you.

We should always evaluate when a patient makes us feel unloved, unwanted or unneeded, because every time you get negative about anybody, especially a patient, he gives you a gift by getting you in touch with your own unfinished business. If you have enough self-worth and self-respect and a feeling of confidence about the role that you play, you will not be devastated when a patient tells you, "No, thank you!" It is very important that people in the health professions learn that, in order not to become "burned out." *You may work eighty hours a week with dying children, with the families of murder victims and suicide and with the greatest tragedies that you can barely conceive, without ever, ever getting burned out as long as you have no unfinished business yourself.*

The Five Natural Emotions

God created man with five natural emotions. They are fear, guilt, anger, jealousy and love. And by the time you are six all the natural emotions have been turned into unnatural ones. Anything on the natural side will maintain your energy and anything on the unnatural side will strain you to such a point that you will call it a burn-out syndrome. How many of you have experienced a burn out? *(several hands)* It does not exist! *(surprised laughter from audience)* A burn-out is as ridiculous as saying, "The Devil made me do it." *(laughter from audience)* The Devil doesn't make you do anything if you don't let him. The burn-out is . . . say that you work in the ICU and you have five patients dying in one day. Then there is the sixth one coming in and it's an hour before you are allowed to leave and you are going to be stuck with that patient and you say, "I can't take another one." And you never share your frustration, your impotence, your rage, your anger, your feelings of unfairness. You are the care giver and you keep a lid on all your frustrations and your negativity because you can't go round sobbing and crying or beating the doctors up. And so you keep this nice, smiling front. And after a while you are just going to explode. And if you don't explode, then you will be totally drained and the next day you will have to call in sick when you are not sick. That is what the burn-out syndrome is.

And if you become natural again I can guarantee you that you can work seventeen hours a day, seven days a week and you will be peppy. Sometimes you get sleepy but you won't get negative.

Learn to respect the five natural emotions and don't turn them into unnatural emotions. I will go very briefly through them.

❧

We have only two natural **fears**: one of falling from high places, and the other one of unexpected loud noises. You can put a little child up here *(indicating the stage)* — any child — and he would not step down because he has a built-in fear of high places.

I am the death-and-dying lady and I am not afraid to die. But if somebody shot a bullet behind me, I would duck so fast that you would be surprised how fast I am.

These are the natural fears of high places and loud noises. You have been given them to keep you from harming your body — they help you to survive, literally.

(Turns to audience): What other fears do you have? *(amusement and silence from audience)* Say a few ones! *(repeats answers*

from audience) Fear of death, what else? Failures. Respirators. Being alone. Rejection. Heights. The unknown. What the neighbors think. Snakes. Rats. Spiders. People *(giggles from audience)*. And so on.

You end up with a million unnatural fears that make life miserable, and then you pass your phobias on to your children and your children's children. As it is stated so beautifully in the Bible, "The sins of your fathers will be passed on to the children and the children's children." That is what is meant by original sin.

You have no idea how many people spend ninety percent of their life's energy and make choices in their daily life based on fear. That is the biggest, biggest problem you have. Because if you have a life without any fears except for the natural ones, you will be able to begin to live fully. In my workshops... you have no idea what kinds of decisions people make based on fear which they are totally unaware of. The fear of what the neighbors think has killed more children than anything else. The fear of not being loved, the fear of being rejected, the fear of not being a good girl or a good boy have caused more children to commit suicide than any other cause in the whole wide world. I want you to go home tonight, and if you have children, try to think for yourself privately: how many "ifs" do you attach to the statement "I love you."

People who have no fears of what the neighbors would say, people who have no fears of not being loved will live a whole, full life.

Very often when I'm standing at the casket of a child the parents say, "Why did I give him such a hard time? Why didn't I see the beauty of this child? Why did I complain that my son played the drums every night? I complained and complained. Tonight I would have given anything in the world to hear him play the drums."

Grief is a natural emotion and one of the greatest gifts that man is given to take care of all the losses in life. How many of you were allowed to cry as little children? If we would allow our children to grieve when they experience the thousand little deaths in their life, they would not end up as grownups full of self-pity. Our children are very often not allowed to grieve. *(Turns to audience):* What were you told when you were crying? *(repeats answers from audience):* "Big boys don't cry." "You are a cry baby." "Go to your room if you cry again." "God, here she goes again!" *(laughter of recognition from audience)* And my favorite, "If you don't stop crying, I will give you something to cry about!" *(laughter of recognition and applause)* Those children will have a tremendous problem later on with anything related to grief, and they often end up with buckets of self-pity.

If a child falls from a tricycle and you as a parent don't make a big fuss out of it but let her cry, then a few seconds later she will be up on her tricycle taking off again. In this way she will prepare herself for life's windstorms. She will not become a sissy. She will become strong because she will not have a pool of repressed tears.

Repressed grief turns into pulmonary problems and asthma. You can stop an asthmatic attack if you help the patient to cry. I am not saying that repressed grief by itself *causes* asthma, but a pool of repressed tears adds enormously to asthma, to pulmonary problems and to GI problems. If you have families with a big history of asthma and help them to get their tears out, they are going to be much better off.

❦

Anger is even worse. Children are not supposed to be angry. But then the natural anger in a child that is raised naturally only takes fifteen seconds, which is long enough to say, "No, mom!"

(Turns to audience) How may of you were spanked, bashed, belted, punished or sent to your room when you were angry as a child? *(silence from audience)* Nobody here in Sweden? *(laughter)* I can't believe that. How many of you were *not ever* punished when you were angry?

Very few children are accepted when they are angry. What the parents need to learn then is that natural anger only lasts for fifteen seconds. Then it's over with and they are ready to move on. But if you are not allowed to be angry and, even worse, if you get spanked, punished or reprimanded, then you will become Hitlers, small and big Hitlers, who are full of rage and revenge and hate. The world is full of them. And I'm using this word specifically because there is a Hitler in all of us. A mini-Hitler or a maxi-Hitler.

If you, as a grownup, have the courage to get in touch with your own repressed anger from way back since you were a child, and get in touch with how many times you have been mad at somebody or angry at somebody for more than fifteen seconds, then you will get in touch with something that has been repressed which we call rage, hate and revenge. This is physically the worst kind of unfinished business you can carry with you, because if you keep those repressed feelings inside of you for any extended period of time they will eventually affect your physical quadrant and will lead to ill health.

Hate, which is distorted anger, is a great killer in terms of physical illness. Every unnatural emotion has its physical equivalent: a coronary is an expression of repressed fear and anger. If you are a member of a family genetically inclined to coronaries at age forty and you are a man approaching that age and you know it's like a knife over your head, then come to one of my workshops and I will help you get rid of your anger and fear. You have never imagined what is inside of you — it is like a pressure cooker that is ready to erupt. Get rid of your fear and anger and in spite of the genetic probability of having a coronary at a young age you will add years to your life span. It is the repressed negative emotions that are the great killers in our society.

Billy

I once made a house call to an eight-year-old dying child. The parents were hovering over him and in the same room there was another little child sitting near the window all by himself like he didn't belong to the family. I presumed that he was a visiting neighbor. Nobody included him, nobody talked to him, nobody introduced him to me. It was like he was nonexistent. If you see the patients in their home you learn a lot. I too ignored him totally and played into the scheme of this family.

In the course of the conversation I realized that this must be Billy, the brother of the sick child. He was about seven years old. Before I left, I asked him to draw a picture and I realized that the dying boy had no problems but *he*, Billy, had more problems than the rest of the family together. I asked him what his big problem was and he couldn't tell me in plain English. I asked him to draw another picture, and then I was able to talk to him as a result of his own picture.

As I was leaving when my house call was finished I got up and said to Billy, "I want *you* to walk me to the door." He jumped up and said, "Me?" I said, "You, and you alone." And I gave the mother what I call the "eagle eye" *(laughter from audience)* which means, "You stay right where you are and you are not going to come out and snoop on what I'm doing with that little boy." She got the message and we walked to the door. And at the door he grabbed my hand, and just as he closed the door enough, not to be visible to the parents, he looked at me and said, "I guess you know that I have asthma." And I blurted out (I'm most of the time not thinking first), "That doesn't surprise me."

By then we were at the car and we sat in the front seat and we closed the door half way so the snooping parents couldn't peek.

I said, "So you have asthma!" And he said very sadly, "I guess it's not good enough." And I said, "Not good enough?" He said very matter of factly, "My brother gets electric train sets, he gets trips to Disneyland, there is nothing that they would not do for him. But when I wanted a football my dad said no. And when I asked him how come, he got very angry and said, 'Would you rather have cancer?'"

Do you understand the logical thinking of those parents? Do you understand the boy's tragedy?

Children take everything literally. It is no wonder that some children develop psychosomatic symptoms. If we, the grownups, tell them quite explicitly, "If you have cancer you can get anything, but if you are well, don't make any demands on us," then it is understandable that such a child will grow up with tremendous rage, hate, revenge and self-pity. He may think something like this, "If my brother gets bigger toys the more sick he gets, maybe I'm not sick enough, and I have to get more sick." That is the beginning of psychosomatic illness. Then he develops asthma, and the more sick he becomes, the bigger the gift he thinks that he will get. Later on, he may become a big, big manipulator because anytime he wants something he will have a dramatic heart attack or asthma attack.

He may also wish that his brother will die quickly so that life will become normal again and so that he will again get a little slice of the pie. That, of course, will make him feel very guilty.

We see this kind of unnatural behavior very often. You can help parents to understand that they have to really watch what they tell little children because they take everything so literally. And you can help this little child to grieve for all the things that he didn't get and also that he never got enough attention. He would be helped if he is allowed to grieve and if a neighbor or a clergyman or a friend or anybody takes this healthy little boy out and gives him special attention. They can do a lot of preventive medicine and preventive psychiatry by making him understand that he doesn't have to have cancer in order to be loved. All children need love, and if they get it they will not have to develop asthma in order to compete with a brother who has cancer.

It is quite a different thing with children who have been loved unconditionally and have been allowed to express their natural anger. When they are dying they will be able to tell you in a very few minutes when they have had enough of the treatment. Their intuitive quadrant knows when they are only going to live a few days more, and they will tell mommy or daddy or a doctor or a nurse, or someone else they trust, "It is time now for me to go home." If you can hear that, you will never miss the chance when the patient tells you, "I have a few days to live. I need to go home now." And you would love to hear that, and you would then easily find the courage to stop the chemotherapy or whatever it is you have initiated, because you would already know that the patient knows that he is not going to live through it.

The beauty in working with dying patients — if you are ready to get rid of your own blocks, your own unfinished business — is that you will be able to *hear* the intuitive quadrant of your patient speaking. In all my twenty years of working with dying patients, grownups and children, I have never had a patient who did not know that he was dying. That includes five-year-old children, who, from the intellectual quadrant, have no idea what is wrong with them. Still they can tell you not only what is wrong with them — not in scientific language but in drawings — but they also can tell you when death is near. *If* you can hear that, *if* the parents do not project their own needs, *if* the doctor allows himself to know that patients know more about themselves than he does, then you will never have a problem with the artificial prolongation of life when it is not helpful. I will give you a very practical example of that when I have finished talking about the natural emotions.

Jealousy is a natural emotion, very natural, very positive. It helps little children to emulate, to copy older children learning how to ski, ice skate, play the flute, read a book. If you belittle them in their natural jealousy, it turns into very ugly envy and competition. If this form of natural jealousy is knocked and belittled, it turns the mind into a state of an unending competition.

***

Love is the biggest problem of them all, a problem that pushes our world almost to self-destruction. If we do not understand love, we run into problems, not only with dying patients but also with the living. Love consists of two aspects. One of them is holding, hugging, touching, and giving physical security. And the other one, the most important part that is forgotten by most people, is the courage to say "no;" to say "NO" in capital letters to somebody you love. If you cannot say no, it is a sign that you have too much fear, shame or guilt within you. A mother who ties shoelaces for her child until he is twelve years old doesn't give him love but the opposite because she cannot say "no" to him.

There is also another way of saying "no" that parents have to learn. Parents who love a child *so* much that they don't let him cross the street by himself and don't let him stay away with friends overnight and don't allow him to go anywhere, those parents have not learned to say "no" to *their own* needs. They do not express love for their child by stopping him. On the contrary, they project their own fears and their own unfinished business onto him.

If you have too much fear, shame and guilt to say "no" to your children or to yourself, you will raise a generation of cripples, depriving them from living, and depriving yourself of the greatest experience of your life.

Jeffy

When you work with dying children, you experience what the effects of lack of love are all about. And you go home and look at your own children and try to practice what dying children teach you. My best and briefest example is nine-year-old Jeffy, who had leukemia for six out of his nine years in life. He was in and out of the hospital. He was a very sick boy when I saw him for the last time in the hospital. He had central nervous system involvement. He was like a drunk little man. His skin was very pale, almost discolored. He was barely able to stand on his feet. He had lost his hair many, many times with chemotherapy. He could not even look at the injection needles any more, and everything was too painful for him.

I was very aware that this child had a few weeks, at the most, to live. After you take care of a family with such a child for six years out of his nine years, you naturally become part of it.

That very day it was a very young, new physician who came on his rounds. As I walked in I heard him say to Jeffy's parents, "We are going to try another chemotherapy."

I asked the parents and the physicians if they had asked Jeffy, if *he* was willing to take another series of treatment. As the parents loved him unconditionally, they were able to allow me to ask this question to Jeffy in their presence. Jeffy gave me a most beautiful answer in the way children speak. He very simply said, "I don't understand you grownups, why you have to make us children so sick to get us well?"

We talked about it. This was Jeffy's way of expressing the natural fifteen seconds of anger. This child had enough self-worth, inner authority and self-love to have the courage to say, "No thank you," which was what Jeffy said. The parents were able to hear it, respect it and accept it.

Then I wanted to say good-bye to Jeffy. But Jeffy said, "No. I want to be sure that I am taken home today." If a child tells you, "Take me home *today*," there is a sense of great urgency, and we try *not* to postpone it. Therefore I asked the parents if they were willing to take him home. The parents had enough love and courage to do that.

And again I wanted to say good bye. But Jeffy, like all children who are still terribly honest and simple, said to me, "I want *you* to come home with me."

I looked at my watch, which in the symbolic, nonverbal language means, "You know, I really don't have the time to go home with all my children." Without my saying anything in words, he understood instantly and said, "Don't worry, it will only take ten minutes."

I went home with him, knowing that in the next ten minutes at home Jeffy would finish his unfinished business. We drove home — the parents, Jeffy and I. We drove into the driveway, opening the garage.

We are in the garage and get out of the car. Jeffy says very matter-of-factly to his father, "Take my bicycle down from the wall."

Jeffy had a brand new bicycle that was hanging on two hooks inside the garage wall. For a long time the dream of his life had been to be able, once in his lifetime, to ride around the block on a bicycle. And so his father had bought him a beautiful bicycle. But because of his illness he had never been able to ride it. It had been hanging there on its hooks for three years.

Now Jeffy asked his dad to take it down. With tears in his eyes he asked him to put the training wheels on the bicycle. I do not know if you appreciate how much humility it takes for a nine-year-old boy to ask for training wheels, usually used only by very little children.

And the father, with tears in his eyes, put the training wheels on his son's bicycle. Jeffy was like a drunk man, barely able to stand on his feet.

When the father was finished with the training wheels, Jeffy took one look at me and said, "And *you* Doctor Ross, you are here to hold my mom back."

Jeffy knew that his mom had one problem, one unfinished business. She was not yet able to learn the love that can say "no" to her own needs. Her biggest need was to lift up her very sick child on the bicycle like a two-year-old, to hold onto him and to run with him around the block. And thus she would have cheated him out of the greatest victory of his life.

Therefore I held mom back, and her husband held *me* back. We held each other back and learned the hard way how painful and difficult it sometimes is in the face of a very vulnerable, terminally ill child to allow him the victory and the risk to fall and hurt and bleed.

He drove off.

After an eternity he came back, the proudest man you have ever seen. He was beaming from one ear to the other. He looked like somebody who had won the gold medal in the Olympics.

He very proudly came off the bicycle and asked his father with *great* authority and sense of pride to take the training wheels off and to carry the bicycle into his bedroom.

And then very unsentimentally, very beautifully, very straightforwardly he turned to me and said, "And you, Dr. Ross, you can go home now." He kept his promise that it would only take ten minutes of my time.

But he also gave me the greatest gift that I was able to witness: his great victory, the fulfillment of an incredible dream. This would *never* have been possible had we kept him in the hospital.

Two weeks later his mother called me up and said, "I have to tell you the end of the story."

After I had left, Jeffy said, "When my brother comes home from school" — his brother was Dougy, a first grader — "you send him upstairs, but no grown-ups, please." That is again the "no thank you." And they respected that.

Dougy came home and was sent up to his brother. When he, a while later, came down again, he refused to tell his parents what he and his brother had been talking about.

It was only two weeks later that he was allowed to tell us what had happened during that visit.

Jeff had told Dougy that he wanted the pleasure of personally giving him his most beloved bicycle. But he could not wait another two weeks until it was

Dougy's birthday, because by then he would be dead. Therefore he wanted to give it to him now, but only under one condition: that Dougy would *never* use those damned training wheels *(laughter from audience)*. This was another expression of fifteen seconds of anger.

Jeffy died a week later. Dougy had his birthday another week later and was then allowed to share with us the end of the story: how a nine-year-old child finished his unfinished business.

And I hope you realize that the parents had a lot of grief, but no grief *work,* no fear, no guilt, no shame, "Oh my God, if we had only been able and willing to hear him."

They had the memory of this ride around the block and that beaming face of Jeffy, who was able to achieve his great victory over something that most of us, unfortunately, take all too for granted.

Children know what they need. Children know when the time is close. Children share with you their unfinished business. And it is only your own fear and your own guilt and your own shame and your own clinging on that prevents you from hearing it. And by doing so you cheat yourself out of sacred moments like this one.

My next brief example of unfinished business has nothing to do with hate or unresolved grief work. It has to do with taking the good things for granted... *(interrupts herself)* By the way, how many of you have not talked to your mother-in-law for ten years or more? *(amusement in audience)* I do not expect public confessions *(laughter)* but at least ask yourself: why do I treat people who don't approve of me... why do I need to treat them with the revenge of silence?

If that mother-in-law of yours dies tomorrow, you will spend a fortune at the florist, and that only helps the florist *(laughter)*. But if tomorrow you feel that ten years of punishment is enough, then you may go and pick some flowers and give them to her. But do not expect her to love you or thank you. She may even throw them in your face, but *you* will have given her your peace offering. If she then dies the next day you will have grief but no grief work. Grief is natural and a God-given gift. Grief work is, "If I had only . . ."

But unfinished business is not only un-expressed grief, anger, jealousy, and nega-tive things. Unfinished business can bother you just as much if you have had positive experiences which you have not shared with your fellow man. A teacher, for example, who has been very influen-tial in your life and has really given your life sense and purpose and direction, and you never took the time to say thank you to him, and then suddenly he dies and you think, "God, it would have been nice if I had written him a letter."

Maybe the best and briefest example of this kind of unfinished business which can haunt you for years and years after-wards is a letter that a young girl wrote about Viet Nam. It is an "If I had only...":

Remember the day I borrowed your brand new car and I dented it?

I thought you'd kill me, but you didn't.

Remember the time I dragged you to the beach and you said it would rain and it did?

I thought you'd say, "I told you so," but you didn't.

Remember the time I flirted with all the guys to make you jealous and you were?

I thought that you'd leave me, but you didn't.

And the time I spilled blueberry pie over your brand new trousers?

I thought you'd drop me for sure, but you didn't.

And the time I forgot to tell you the dance was formal and you showed up in blue jeans?

I thought you'd smack me, but you didn't.

There were so many things that I wanted to make up to you when you returned from Viet Nam.

But you didn't.

I hope that if you have had a Grandma or a kindergarten teacher or anybody who was really special to you — it doesn't have to be in your family — that you say all these things before you hear that he or she has died. That too is unfinished business.

When you take the courage to become honest again, as honest as children are, you will begin to see that you have the courage to evaluate and to look honestly on your own unfinished business. Get rid of it so that you can become whole again. Then your intuitive, spiritual quadrant will emerge. You don't have to do anything for it except to get rid of your negativity. When you have developed this, your life will change drastically.

You will then always hear your patients. You will always hear when they need help. You will always hear from *whom* they need help — this is not always you. You will also hear what it is that they need in order to finish whatever they have not yet finished.

Working with dying patients then becomes an incredible blessing. And it will never ever lead to a burn-out, because each time you react, each time you find some little unfinished business popping up from time to time like a weed in the garden, you will know that you have to weed your garden again.

When you finish your unfinished business, all your repressed hate and greed and grief work and all the negative stuff that ruins not only your life, but also your health, you will find that it no longer matters whether you die at twenty or fifty or ninety, and then you will have nothing to be worried about.

When you discover that same source of inner knowledge within other people, with people who die a sudden death, you will find that even children who have been murdered, even children who are hit by a car and die a sudden, unexpected death, know inside not only *that* they will die but also *how* they will die.

It is important that you know that the younger you are the more you know. The less you know up here *(indicating head)* the more you know here *(indicating intuitive quadrant)* — almost, it is not totally so. And people who are intellectually hypertrophic... Do you understand what I mean by that? You go to school for years and years and years and in that process you lose your intuition, because you learn to analyze everything up here *(head)*, and you forget that you know far more in here *(intuition)*. You get into trouble with your intellectual quadrant and you need to really learn how to keep it in harmony with your intuitive quadrant. That is very difficult.

Do you hear what I am trying to say to you? Finishing your own unfinished business is the only way that you can bring about a change in the world. And I will briefly talk as a psychiatrist because it is very important that you heal the world soon, before it is too late: *you have to understand that you cannot heal the world without healing yourself first.*

(A man in the audience asks a question.) Did everybody hear the question? *("No!")* He asked how we can deal with conflicts with the society, how the society could work with dying patients, so that we don't have to work only on an individual level like I do. *You* are the society! In 1968, I was the only person who talked to dying patients in the United States and who taught it in medical schools and theological seminaries. And in the last years we have had 125,000 courses every year in the United States alone. It starts with one person, and you can start it. You have started it already.

We had one hospice in 1970. And last year we had 100 hospices coming up in one year in California alone. They are coming up like "Chicken Delights." I hope you understand what I mean. This is not good. It is very *en vogue* right now. Everybody starts hospices because they get government money, and it's politically wise to do it. But if something is not done out of love, unconditional love, but instead out of profit or prestige or as an ego trip, then it is not worth it. So if ten thousand people here in Sweden start having the courage to take the patients home to die, helping your neighbors to take their husband or their child home, then it would take very few people to do this work. And as long as you do it free of charge, without expectations of starting a famous "Death & Dying Center" or whatever non-positive motivations you might have, you will do a wonderful job with your dying patients. It takes one or two people who are not afraid to start it. And you may experience a lot of abuse, and a lot of hostility at some times, but the fruit of your labor is worthwhile. That is really all I can say about it.

(Question from audience, "What do you say to a child whose mother has committed suicide?") We see many children whose mothers have committed suicide. You do not preach to them, you do not say anything *to* them. You let the child draw a picture and let him share with you what it means to him, and give him a safe place where

he can externalize his rage, his anger, his sense of unfairness, and his tremendous grief. And then, when he has poured out all that anguish and anger, only then we begin to help him to understand why some people find this the only solution. And we do it with compassion. Not with judgment.

But you cannot do that until you have helped him to externalize his rage, his impotence, his anger, and for this you need a very safe place. That is what we do in our workshops. All people in our workshops have pains like that.

───────

(Elisabeth invites the audience to ask more questions specifically about children and death before she will move on to the next subject for the evening which is life after death. Nevertheless, a lot of people in the audience start asking questions about life after death. For a while though, she only answers questions about children and death and the audience becomes more and more impatient to hear about life after death. Elisabeth picks

up these feelings from the audience and the following is her response to those feelings.)

(Impatient question from audience, "When are you going to talk about life after death?" Elisabeth answers.)

As soon as the earthly business is finished *(reluctant laughs from audience).*

There are a lot of people who want to know a lot about life after death and they do not understand that if you live fully and in harmony, without negativity and without unfinished business, you will get *your own* experiences. To live this way is the only way to become totally open on the intuitive and spiritual quadrant. I have never myself done *anything* to achieve all my mystical experiences. I can't even sit still to meditate. I eat meat, I drink coffee, I smoke, I have never been to India, I don't have a Guru or a Baba *(laughs from audience)* and I have had every... *(applause)* ... and I have had every mystical experience that you could ever dream of ever getting in your life.

And the only thing that I would like to convey to you is that you do not need drugs, you do not need to go to India, you do not need a Guru or a Baba or outside people who tell you how to do it. If you are ready for spiritual experiences and you are not afraid you will get them yourself.

If you are not ready for them, you will not believe what I tell you. But on the other hand, if you *know* already, then they could hang you by your toe nails and still you would know.

Do you see the difference between *knowing* something and *believing* something? Once you know, no matter what they do to you, you will know that death does not exist. I have collected twenty-thousand cases of near death experiences and I stopped collecting them because I had the illusion that it was my job to tell people that death does not exist.

I believed that it was of utmost importance to tell people what happens at the moment of death, and I discovered very soon *(with just a hint of pain in her voice)* — and the price wasn't terribly low —that those who are ready to listen know it anyway, just the way my children — when they are ready for it — know that they are dying. On the other hand, those who do *not* believe it, those people you could give one-million examples and they would *still* tell you it's only a result of oxygen deprivation. But this doesn't really matter because after they die, they will know it anyway *(amusement, giggles and applause from audience)*. If they need to rationalize those things away, that is their problem.

The only Hitler I want to keep inside of me is that when those people who gave me a hard time as a result of publicly speaking about the near-death experience, make the transition, I am gonna to sit there, and I'm gonna watch their surprised faces, and I'm gonna... *(laughter from audience)*... use symbolic, nonverbal language! *(laughter and applause)*

I'm going to tell you now anyway what you need to know, if it helps.

It is very important to me that people who do research on life after death do it in as systematic and as scientific a way as there is. Because if you don't use the right language, it sounds very coo-coo.

I have worked with dying patients for the last twenty years and when I started this work I must say that I was neither very interested in life after death nor did I have any really clear picture of the definition of death except naturally for those that the science of medicine has defined. When you study the definition of death, you see that it only includes the death of the physical body as if man only consisted of the cocoon.

I was one of those physicians, scientists, who did not ever question that. But in the 1960s it started to become very difficult to be a physician with the transplants coming and the deep freeze societies and people believing that we can conquer death with money and technology. They froze people at the moment of death and promised to defrost them "twenty years from now" when there might be a cure for cancer. People spent $9,000 a year with the illusion that their next of kin could be defrosted alive. It was like the peak of arrogance and stupidity, if you don't mind my saying so. It was ignorance, grandiosity, a denial of our own mortality, a denial of the origin from where we came. It was a denial that life has a purpose, and that life in this physical world does not *have* to last forever, it was a denial of the fact that the quality of life is far more important than the years — the quantity of life.

And in those days it became extremely difficult to be a physician because in the United States... I remember one day when we had twelve parents in the waiting room for *one* child to be saved. We had to dialyze in those days, but we didn't have enough equipment, and physicians had to choose only one out of twelve children for dialysis. Which one deserved most to live?

It was a terrible nightmare.

Then they also came up with liver transplants and heart transplants and even started to talk about brain transplants. And in parallel the law suits started to come in, since our materialism has reached a point where people sue each other where the issue of prolongation has raised many, many difficult problems. Also we can be sued for either attempting to take an organ too early out of a person when the family claims that they are still alive, or when we wait too long and perhaps often prolong the life unnecessarily.

The life insurance companies have also added to this problem in that in a family accident it is sometimes of vital importance to know who in a family died first, even if it is only a matter of minutes. Again the issue is money and who the beneficiaries would be.

Needless to say, all these issues would have touched me very little had it not been for my own very subjective experiences at the bedside of my own dying patients. Being a skeptical semi-believer to put it mildly, and not interested in issues of life after death, I could not help but be impressed by several observations which occurred so frequently that I began to wonder why nobody ever had studied the *real* issues of death — not for any special scientific reasons, not to cover lawsuits, needless to say, but simply out of sheer natural curiosity.

One day, when several lawsuits had come into the hospital, I had a discussion with the beautiful black minister with whom I started the old Death and Dying seminars at the University of Chicago. I loved him very dearly, and with him I had had this super-ideal symbiosis. This day he philosophized with me on what we could do to bring medicine back to where it used to be. And I was an old fashioned country doctor from Switzerland so I had lots of ideals about my profession. And we decided that the real problem was that we don't have a definition of death.

Man has existed for forty-seven million years and has been in his present existence, which includes the facet of divinity, for seven million years. Every day people die all over the world and yet in a society that is able to send a man to the moon and bring him back alive and safe, we have never put any efforts into the study of an updated and total definition of human death. Isn't that peculiar?

We have definitions, but they all have exceptions, like if you have barbiturates or if you are very cold you can have a flat EEG and can still be brought back to a normal life without brain damage. And any definition that has exceptions is obviously not the final definition. And so in my juvenile enthusiasm I said to this minister, "I'm going to promise God that I live long enough to find a definition of death." It was a very naive, childlike fantasy to think that if we had a definition of death then the lawsuits would disappear and we could go back to being healers and physicians.

And because I always had lots of problems with other ministers who talk a lot and don't believe what they are saying and don't live it themselves, I challenged this one and said, "You guys, you are always up on the pulpit and you say 'Ask and you will be given'. I'm gonna ask you now: help me to do research on death."

The Near-Death Experience

It is said somewhere, "Ask and you will be given. Knock and it will be open." Or, in a different language, "A teacher will appear when the student is ready." This proved to be very true. Within one week after raising this important question and making a commitment to finding an answer to it, we were visited by nurses who shared with us the experience of a woman, a Mrs. Schwartz, who had been in the intensive care unit fifteen times.

Each time this woman was expected to die, and yet each time she was able to walk out of the intensive care unit to live for another few weeks or months. She was, as we would call it now, our first case of a near-death experience.

This occurred simultaneously with my increasing sensitivity and observation of other unexplained phenomena at the time when my own patients were very, very close to death. Many of them began to "hallucinate" the presence of loved ones with whom they apparently had some form of communication but whom I, personally, was neither able to see nor hear.

I was also quite aware that even the angriest and most difficult patients, very shortly before death, begin to deeply relax, have a sense of serenity around them, and begin to be pain free in spite of, perhaps, a cancer-ridden body full of metastases. Also, at the moment after death, their facial features expressed an incredible sense of peace and equanimity and serenity which I could not comprehend since it was often a death that occurred during a stage of anger, bargaining or depression.

My third and perhaps most subjective observation was the fact that I have always been very close to my patients and allowed myself to get deeply and lovingly involved with them. They touched my life and I touched their lives in a very intimate, meaningful way. Yet within minutes after the death of a patient I had no feelings for him or her, and I often wondered if there was something wrong with me. When I looked at the body, it appeared to me similar to a winter coat, shed with the occurrence of spring, not needed any more. I had this incredible, clear image of a shell, and my beloved patient was no longer in there.

We discovered that it is possible to do research on life after death. This discovery was, for me, an incredibly moving experience, and I will simply summarize what we have learned in the last many, many years, studying this phenomenon, which is called — for the time being — the near-death experience.

Our dream was to collect twenty cases. We have now twenty-thousand cases. We never published them and I'm glad we never did because what we found out when we started to look for cases was that there were lots of people who were willing to share with us, but they always started their sharing by saying, "Dr. Ross, I will share something with you if you promise not to tell it to another human being." They were almost paranoid about it. Because when they came back after having had this glorious experience which for them was very sacred, very private, and shared it with people, they got a nice little pat on their back and were told, "Well, you were under drugs," or "It is very normal that people hallucinate at moments like this."

They were also given psychiatric labels which, of course, made them very angry or depressed. We always need to label things that we don't understand. There are many things that we don't know yet. But that doesn't mean that they don't exist.

We collected these cases not only from the United States but also Australia and Canada; the youngest patient is a two-year-old child, the oldest a ninety-seven year old man. We have people from different cultural and religious backgrounds including Eskimos, original Hawaiians, aborigines from Australia, Hindus, Buddhists, Protestants, Catholics, Jews, and several people without any religious identification, including a few who called themselves agnostics or atheists. It was important for us to collect data from the greatest possible variety of people from different religious and cultural backgrounds, as we wanted to be very sure not only that our material was not contaminated, but that it was a uniquely *human* experience, and that it had nothing to do with early conditioning, religious or otherwise.

Also relevant is the fact that they had these experiences after an accident, murder attempt, suicide attempt or a slow lingering death. Over half of our cases have been sudden death experiences. In these cases the patients have not been able to prepare themselves for, or anticipate, an experience.

Whoever among you is ready to hear the truth will not have to look far in order to get your own cases. If children sense your motivation, they will share their knowledge freely. But if you are out to be negative, they will pick it up very quickly and they will not share anything with you. I am not exaggerating when I say to you: If you can get rid of your own negativity, then everything will be open for you and the patients will sense it, and they will share with you. And you will find that they will give you all the knowledge that you need, that you are ready for — but not more. And you know, some of you are in high school and some of you are only in first grade. You will always get what you need, but you will not always get what you want. That is a universal law.

***

We say that you are not really you, the way you look at yourself in the mirror and the way you worry every day that you are too fat or too flat-chested or your hips are to fat or you have too many wrinkles. That is *totally* irrelevant. You are beautiful because you are you, because you are unique. There are billions of people and no two are alike. Not even identical triplets. And I am an identical triplet *(she laughs a little)*.

In memory of the children in Auschwitz and Maidanek, we are using the model of the cocoon and the butterfly. We say that you are like the cocoon of a butterfly. The cocoon is what you see in a mirror. It is only a temporary housing of your *real* you. When this cocoon gets damaged beyond repair, you die, and what happens is that the cocoon, which is created of physical energy, will — symbolically speaking — relieve the butterfly.

You have the same subjective experience of death whether the destruction of the cocoon happens through homicide, suicide, sudden death or slow lingering death. The cause of death does not alter the subjective experience of the moment of death.

The immortal part of you will be released out of your physical shell. What you bury or cremate is not you, it's only the cocoon. That is very important to understand. When we work with little children, we show them how this happens. At that moment you will be very beautiful. Much more beautiful than you see yourself now. You will be perfect. Mutilations like mastectomies and amputations do not follow you into death. But the body you now have is no longer created by physical energy but psychic energy.

The Common Denominators

We will share with you the three common denominators that we have found.

When we leave the physical body there will be a total absence of panic, fear or anxiety. We will have all awareness. Awareness is higher than consciousness because it also includes everything that's going on in the environment where our physical body is shed: what people in the vicinity of our body are thinking, what kind of excuses they use to lie to themselves and things like that.

We will always experience a physical wholeness. We will be totally aware of the environment in which the accident or death takes place, whether this is a hospital room, our own bedroom after a coronary, or the scene of a car accident or a plane crash. We will be quite aware of the people who work in the resuscitation team or the rescue team trying to extricate the body from a car wreck. We will watch this at a distance of a few feet in a rather detached state of mind, if I may use the word "mind," though we are no longer connected with the mind or with a functioning brain at this moment in most cases. This all occurs at a time when brain-wave tests give no signs of brain activities, and very often at the time when physicians find no signs of life whatsoever.

Our second body, which we experience at this time, is not a physical body, but an ethereal body, and we will talk later on about the differences between physical, psychic and spiritual energy, which create these forms.

It is understandable that many of our patients who have been successfully resuscitated are not always grateful when their butterfly is squashed back into the cocoon, since with the revival of our bodily functions we also have to accept the pains and the handicaps that go with it.

In the state of the ethereal body we have no pain and no handicaps. Many of my colleagues wondered if this is not simply a projection of our wishful thinking, which would be very understandable and comprehensible. If anyone has been paralyzed, mute, blind or handicapped for many years, they may be looking forward to a time when the suffering is ended. But it is very easy to evaluate whether this is a projection of wishful thinking or not.

Number one: half of our cases have been sudden, unexpected accidents or near-death experiences where people were unable to foresee what was going to hit them, as in the case of a hit-and-run driver who amputated the legs of one of our patients. And yet, when he was out of his physical body, he saw his amputated leg on the highway and at the same time was fully aware of having both of his legs on his ethereal, perfect and whole body. So we cannot assume that he had previous knowledge of the loss of his legs and would therefore project, in his own wishful thinking, that he was able to walk again.

Number two: there is also a much simpler way to rule out the projection of wishful thinking. That is to ask blind people who do not even have light perception to share with us what it was like when they had this near death experience. If it were just a dream fulfillment those people would not be able to give accurate details of their surroundings.

We have questioned several totally blind people who were able to share with us in their near death experience and they were not only able to tell us who came into the room first, who worked on the resuscitation, but they were also able to give minute details of the attire and the clothing of all the people present, something a totally blind person, the victim of wishful thinking, would never be able to do.

You need to understand that this is not the resurrection that is described in Christian teaching. The body we have during a near death experience is a very temporary form, created out of psychic energy to help you make the experience of death a pleasant reunion, and not a scary, frightening, horrifying experience.

Once we have gone through something that symbolizes a transition — it is culturally determined and can be a gate or a bridge or a tunnel — we begin to see a light. It is a light that is beyond any description. It is whiter than white, lighter than light, and when we come closer to it, we will be totally wrapped in unconditional love. If we have ever, ever, ever experienced that, we can never, ever again be afraid of death. Death is not scary. It is what we make out of life that is the problem.

People who have seen this light have for, a glimpse of a moment, *all* knowledge. Unfortunately, if they have to come back — if it is a *near* death experience — they forget a lot of it. But what many of them remember is, I think, the only thing that we should be aware of, and that is that our total life is our own responsibility, that we cannot criticize and blame and judge and hate. We, and we alone are responsible for the sum total of our physical life. That realization changes a lot of our priorities.

In the presence of this incredible light, which people call "Christ" or "God" or

"Love" or "Light" depending on where they come from, we will be held responsible for everything we have done. And we will then understand how often we have not taken the highest choice and how we have suffered the consequences of our choices.

Here we will know that the absolutely only thing that matters is love. Everything else, our achievements, degrees, the money we made, how many mink coats we had, is totally irrelevant. It will also be understood that *what* we do is not important. The only thing that matters is *how* we do what we do. And the only thing that matters is that we do what we do with love.

In this total, unconditional love we will have to review not only every deed of our life, but also every thought and every word of our total existence. And we will have all knowledge. That means that we will know how every thought, word and deed and choice of our total life has affected others. Our life is literally nothing but a school, where we are tested, where we are put through the tumbler. And it is *our* choice, and no one else's choice, whether we come out of the tumbler crushed or polished.

෨෨෨෨෨

You can collect thousands of cases of near-death experiences — if you need to. But we became very aware that it is not necessary to do that. Because those who want to believe will believe, those who want to know will find out — if they so wish — and those who are not ready for it — if you have a hundred-and-fifty-thousand cases, they will come up with a hundred-and-fifty-thousand rationalizations. And that is their problem.

What I need to say before I end is that Moody's first book, *Life after Life*, which is the only one that is correct, is helpful, but it will not tell you what death is all about, because those are all *near*-death experiences.

After we shed our physical body, which is *physical* energy, we create a secondary, perfect body — meaning without blindness, without amputations, without mastectomies, without defects — with *psychic* energy, which is man-created and manipulated by man, by our mind.

When we are permanently dead, if I can use such horrible language, irreversibly dead, then we will take on a different form that is the form that we have before birth and after death. And that is when we, in Moody's language, go through the tunnel toward the light. That light is pure *spiritual* energy. Spiritual energy is the only energy form in this Universe that cannot be manipulated by man.

Those of you who do research in this field or study higher consciousness or want to understand more about the intricate design of life have to learn two essential things. The first thing is the difference between *real* and *reality*. And the second is the differences between physical, psychic and spiritual energy. Because you are going to read papers by scientists who share with you the existence of

Satan and of Hell and of nightmarish and scary and very real nightmares that especially coronary patients, who are frightened, experience. Those nightmares are *real* but not *reality*. They are projections of one's own fears and are very real but not reality.

Psychic energy is, as I mentioned, the creation of man. It is meant as a gift, and it is up to you to turn this gift into nightmares and ugly negative things or into blessings. Use your psychic energy to learn how to heal and do not use it to destroy.

Voodoo death is a classical example of using psychic energy to kill those who are afraid of the curse of voodoo. I can kill anybody, if I choose, with psychic energy, with voodoo death, if he is afraid of voodoo. But on the other hand, if all of you would put a curse on me with your own psychic energy, which is very powerful, all your psychic energy in this room could not touch me as long as I have no fear of voodoo. Negativity can only feed on negativity. Raise your children without fear and guilt and help them to get rid of the Hitler in them, so you can create Mother Theresas.

If you are honest again and become like children, you will learn that all it takes is to honestly look at yourself and your own negativity. If you have the courage to get rid of that negativity, you will then become whole, and you will learn unconditional love and discipline. As you practice that and learn that, you will be able to teach it and pass it on to your children.

I think Richard Allen put this very beautifully when he summed up not his own life but the life of his father. His father was to him an example of a man who started very negatively and struggled to get rid of his own negativity and his judgmental attitude and who became a being of total and unconditional love, able to pass it on to his children and his children's children. At the end of his life Richard wrote this poem about the meaning of life:

When you love, give it everything
you have got.

And when you have reached your limit,
  give it more, and forget the pain of it.
Because as you face your death
it is only the love that you have given
and received which will count,
and all the rest:
the accomplishments, the struggle,
                the fights
will be forgotten in your reflection.
And if you have loved well
then it will all have been worth it.
And the joy of it will last you through
                the end.

But if you have not,
death will always come too soon
and be too terrible to face.

I would like to finish with a prayer that is very interdenominational because it was written by American Indians to show you that we are all brothers and sisters. It is a poem that was written hundreds of years ago. It is as true today as it will be in thousands of years in the future.

Let me walk in beauty

and make my eyes ever behold
the red and purple sunset.
Make my hands respect the things you
have made,
and my ears sharp to hear your voice.
Make me wise so that I may understand
the things you have taught my people.
Let me learn the lessons you have hidden
in every leaf and rock.
I seek strength
not to be greater than my brother
but to fight my greatest enemy:
myself.
Make me always ready to come to you
with clean hands and straight eyes.
So when life fades
as a fading sunset
my spirit may come to you without
shame.

Thank you.